P9-CCR-901

INSIDE THE WORLD OF SPORTS

GYMNASTICS

INSIDE THE WORLD OF SPORTS

AUTO RACING

BASEBALL

BASKETBALL

EXTREME SPORTS

FOOTBALL

GOLF

GYMNASTICS

ICE HOCKEY

LACROSSE

SOCCER

TENNIS

TRACK & FIELD

WRESTLING

INSIDE THE WORLD OF SPORTS

GYMNASTICS

by Mason Crest

MASON CREST

Mason Crest
450 Parkway Drive, Suite D
Broomall, Pennsylvania 19008
(866) MCP-BOOK (toll free)

Copyright © 2017 by Mason Crest, an imprint of National Highlights, Inc.
All rights reserved. No part of this publication may be reproduced or transmitted in any form
or by any means, electronic or mechanical, including photocopying, recording, taping
or any information storage and retrieval system, without permission from the publisher.

First printing
9 8 7 6 5 4 3 2 1

ISBN (hardback) 978-1-4222-3462-4
ISBN (series) 978-1-4222-3455-6
ISBN (ebook) 978-1-4222-8424-7

Cataloging-in-Publication Data on file with the Library of Congress

QR CODES AND LINKS TO THIRD-PARTY CONTENT

You may gain access to certain third-party content ("Third-Party Sites") by scanning and using the QR Codes that appear in this publication (the "QR Codes"). We do not operate or control in any respect any information, products, or services on such Third-Party Sites linked to by us via the QR Codes included in this publication, and we assume no responsibility for any materials you may access using the QR Codes. Your use of the QR Codes may be subject to terms, limitations, or restrictions set forth in the applicable terms of use or otherwise established by the owners of the Third-Party Sites. Our linking to such Third-Party Sites via the QR Codes does not imply an endorsement or sponsorship of such Third-Party Sites, or the information, products, or services offered on or through the Third-Party Sites, nor does it imply an endorsement or sponsorship of this publication by the owners of such Third-Party Sites.

CONTENTS

KEY ICONS TO LOOK FOR:

Words to understand: These words with their easy-to-understand definitions will increase the reader's understanding of the text while building vocabulary skills.

Educational Videos: Readers can view videos by scanning our QR codes, providing them with additional educational content to supplement the text. Examples include news coverage, moments in history, speeches, iconic sports moments and much more!

Text-dependent questions: These questions send the reader back to the text for more careful attention to the evidence presented there.

Research projects: Readers are pointed toward areas of further inquiry connected to each chapter. Suggestions are provided for projects that encourage deeper research and analysis.

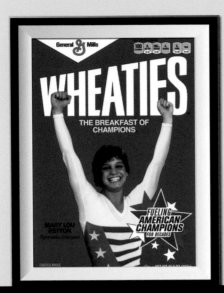

From American stars like Mary Lou Retton and Paul Hamm to international icons like Olga Korbut and Nadia Comăneci, the incredible athletes who compete in gymnastics have thrilled audiences for decades.

CHAPTER 1

GYMNASTICS' GREATEST MOMENTS

How often have you said "Wow!" while watching gymnastics? The flips are often spectacular. The ability of gymnasts to leap into the air and land on a piece of wood that is 4 inches (10 cm) wide is amazing. When a gymnast swinging on a bar with a diameter of 1.1 inches (2.6 cm) takes his hands off, flies into the air, and grabs the bar again as he plunges downward, you just have to say "Wow."

You might also say "Wow!" when you watch a mammoth home run, a bone-jarring tackle, or an incredible dunk. The athletes who perform those feats, however, are generally far taller or heavier than the average human being. Be honest. Don't you think that a feat of athleticism and strength by a man who is smaller than you or a woman who is half your size is more impressive than an athletic feat by someone who is twice your size?

If your answer to this question is "Yes," you should love gymnastics. You should love it even more if you're impressed by grace, charm, poise, theatrics, and showmanship. When you factor in the intangible quality of aesthetic beauty that you almost never find in traditional team sports, you can understand why gymnastics appeals not only to casual sports fans but also to many non-sports fans. The youth and innocence of many of the teenage competitors make the sport even more popular.

Since Olga Korbut enthralled television audiences during the 1972 Summer Olympics with her smile and daring moves, women's gymnastics has been one of the most—if not the most—popular sports in the Olympics. TV ratings show that women, in particular, love to watch gymnastics—men's and women's.

A generation of gymnastics fans got hooked by the perfect routines of Nadia Comăncci in 1976. It was impossible not be charmed by the radiant smile and energetic athleticism of Mary Lou Retton in 1984. These are just some of the greatest moments in the history of the sport—moments from the sport's biggest stage, the Olympic Games, that made us all exclaim, whisper, or mouth the word "Wow!"

Olga Korbut Charms the World

Ludmilla Tourischeva was the Soviet Union's best female gymnast in 1972. She won the gold medal in the individual all-around competition at the 1972 Summer Olympics in Munich, West Germany. Olga Korbut, though, wowed the fans more than Tourischeva could. She was spectacular in helping the Soviets win the team competition gold medal. Only 17 years old, she charmed the crowd and tens of millions of television viewers with her smile, charisma, and youthful exuberance when she executed a daring gold medal-winning balance beam routine and with her tears when she failed in the all-around competition.

Competition in the single apparatus events occurred after the team and individual all-around events. Korbut won gold medals in the floor exercise and balance beam events. The highlight of her performance in the single apparatus events, though, was in the uneven bars. Amazingly, she did a backflip after standing on the top bar and grabbed onto the same bar as she plunged downward. More surprisingly, the judges awarded her only a silver medal. The crowd booed for several minutes and loudly cursed the judges. Korbut won the fans' gold medal.

Watch the video instantly on your mobile device by scanning the QR code next to each video player!

Comăneci Is Perfect

Everyone thought a perfect 10 score was impossible in a gymnastics event at the Olympics. That was true for two reasons in 1976—it had never been done, and the scoreboard only had room for three numbers, with 9.99 being the highest possible score. In an early part of the team competition, 14-year-old Nadia Comăneciof Romania stunned the gymnastics world with her performance on the uneven bars. The judges awarded her a 1.00. At least that is what the scoreboard said. The crowd in Montréal, Canada, was confused until they realized that, in fact, she had scored a 10.00.

Comăneci was so good that a perfect 10 score became a ho-hum routine event during the rest of the 1976 Summer Olympics. Altogether, she had a remarkable seven 10.00 scores—four on the uneven bars and three on the balance beam. She won gold medals in both events and won a third gold in the individual all-around competition. Comăneci also won a silver medal in the team competition and a bronze medal in the floor exercise.

Fujimoto Fights the Pain

Shun Fujimoto won only one Olympic medal during his gymnastics career, but he continues to be a hero in Japan decades after he won the medal. Simply put, Japan would not have won the gold medal in the men's team competition in 1976 if Fujimoto had not demonstrated an unbelievable amount of courage as well as a tremendous commitment to his nation.

What did Fujimoto do? Unbelievably, he competed with a broken right kneecap. He sustained the injury during the floor exercise portion of the team competition, although he didn't know what the injury precisely was because he didn't tell anyone, not even a doctor. Despite severe pain, he scored a 9.5 on the pommel horse. Then, he scored a 9.7 on the rings, landing on the floor after a dismount that included a twisting triple somersault. His knee buckled as he landed. Then, he limped to pick up his gold medal at the podium after Japan edged the Soviet Union by 0.4 points.

Retton Vaults to Fame

West Virginian Mary Lou Retton was no stranger to knee problems leading up to the 1984 Summer Olympics in Los Angeles, California. She had knee surgery just five weeks prior to the competition. With two events left in the individual all-around competition, Retton trailed Ecaterina Szabo of Romania by 0.15 points. Then, she scored a 10 in the floor exercise, while Szabo scored 9.9 on the vault, narrowing the gap to 0.05 points. With one event to go, the vault, Retton needed a 9.95 to tie Szabo and a 10 to win.

Retton raced toward the vault like a sprinter and executed a flawless twisting maneuver called a Tsukahara. Upon landing, she jumped up and down, seemingly knowing that she had won the gold, and waved to the wildly cheering home-country crowd. Yes, Retton had scored another 10 to win the gold. She also won two silver medals and two bronzes during the 1984 Olympics.

Golden Men

As good as Mary Lou Retton was, the United States women had to settle for a silver medal in the team competition in the 1984 Summer Olympics. The men, though, won the nation's second team gold medal in Olympic history. The first was in 1904 when the men won gold in St. Louis.

Like Retton, Tim Daggett scored a 10 in the clutch, executing his horizontal bar routine—the last event of the team competition—perfectly as the United States edged 1983 world champion China by 0.6 points. Teammate Peter Vidmar also excelled, scoring a 9.95 on the horizontal bar. The other gold-medal Americans were Bart Conner, Mitch Gaylord, James Hartung, and Scott Johnson. Vidmar won a gold and silver in individual events, Conner won a gold, Gaylord won a silver and two bronzes, and Daggett won a bronze. The U.S. men have not won a team gold since then.

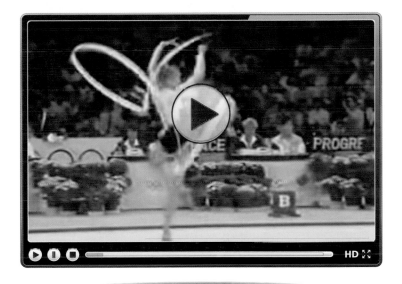

Rhythmic Perfection

It took 48 years for a woman to score a perfect 10 in a women's artistic gymnastics event at the Summer Olympics. Twelve years after Nadia Comäneci's achievement, a woman from the Soviet Union scored a perfect 10 in all six apparatuses only four years after rhythmic gymnastics became an Olympics event.

At the 1988 Summer Olympics in Seoul, South Korea, Marina Lobatch scored a 60 when she won the all-around title. She scored a perfect 10 in the ball, club, hoop, ribbon, and rope events as well as the floor exercise. Lobatch was 18. She retired at age 19.

Strug's Vault

Like Shun Fujimoto, Kerri Strug of Tucson, Arizona, won only one gold medal during her entire Olympics career. Also like Fujimoto, she became a national hero for how she did it. By 1996, women's gymnastics was very popular in the United States, but the U.S. women's team had never won a gold medal in the Olympics. Expectations for that year's team were high with the 1996 Olympics on home soil in Atlanta.

The U.S. women had a big lead going into the final event, the vault, but Strug's five teammates all either stumbled as they completed their routines or fell. Strug was last to perform. On her first vault, she fell and severely hurt her left ankle, scoring just 9.162. With the Russians wrapping up their floor exercise, scores had not yet computed, so no one was sure if that score was good enough to win. Courageously, Strug got up and performed her second vault on two torn ligaments. This time, she landed perfectly, scoring a 9.712. Seconds later, she hopped on her good foot and collapsed. As it turns out, her first score would have been good enough for the U.S. win, but her courage in the moment made Strug an instant heroine. She was hurt so badly that coach Bela Karolyi had to carry her to the medals podium, and she was unable to compete in any individual events. After the Olympics, she was honored at the White House.

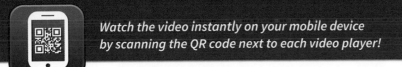

Watch the video instantly on your mobile device
by scanning the QR code next to each video player!

Hamming It Up

Similar to the situation faced by Strug's 1996 women's team, prior to the Atlanta Olympics and going into the 2004 Summer Olympics in Athens, Greece, no American man had ever won the individual all-around title at the Olympics. After the fourth round of the six-round event, there appeared to be zero chance that Wisconsin native Paul Hamm would end that streak. After falling in the vault, he was 12th.

Remarkably, he moved from 12th to 4th after an outstanding performance in the parallel bars. He scored a 9.837. The last round was the horizontal bar. Hamm capped a spectacular routine with a twisting dismount and a perfect landing. He scored another 9.837, the highest score of the event. A gold medalist, Hamm won silver medals in the team competition and also in the horizontal bar. His twin brother Morgan also won a silver in the team competition.

A female acrobat depicted on an Ancient Greek hydria, c. 340-330 BC.

Words to Understand:

assimilated: having adopted the ways of another culture; to fully become part of a different society or country

pentathlon: an athletic contest involving participation by each contestant in five different events

calisthenics: physical exercises done without special equipment

CHAPTER 2

THE ORIGIN OF GYMNASTICS

The origin of the word *gymnastics* is the Greek *gymnazein*, which literally means "to exercise naked." While modern athletes naturally wear clothes during competitions, ancient Grecians looked at these nude exercises, which included running, jumping, tumbling, and even dismounting horses, as a sort of early physical education class. Greeks valued physical fitness but also used the activity to train young soldiers for combat. For both reasons, gymnastics was an essential part of any Greek boy's education, and in fact, the first gymnasiums were educational centers where students worked not only on gymnastics but also math and music.

THE RISE AND FALL

In the centuries that followed, as Romans slowly **assimilated** themselves into what once were Greek territories, the gymnasiums morphed into training facilities exclusively for warfare preparation. The gymnastic exercises themselves survived, edging closer to becoming more formal sporting events. As the Roman Empire fell, however, so too did the popularity of many of these events, and it would be centuries before the world took serious interest in gymnastics as a sport again.

Everything changed in 1774 when a Prussian schoolmaster named Johann Bernhard Basedow introduced a number of physical exercises for the Philanthropinum, a new, forward-thinking school he developed. Basedow's focus on physical education and games was one of many reforms that caught on throughout the Germanic part of the world, and several similar schools opened in the years that followed.

This female athlete performs a backbend. She wears only a diadem (headband) and shoes. Etruscans loved to incorporate human figures, including those of athletes, into their everyday objects.

EVENTS TAKE SHAPE

With physical training growing on a foundation of education, a man named Johann Christoph Friedrich GutsMuths developed the first complete course book for gymnastics, detailing not only the Greek **pentathlon** but also other exercises based on climbing, dancing, jumping, running, swimming, throwing, and walking. His work has earned him recognition as the "Grandfather of Gymnastics."

Johann Christoph Friedrich GutsMuths

Around that same time, Friedrich Ludwig Jahn of Germany also nudged the sport toward its current form, taking existing ideas and exercises and transforming them into some of the events that now are essential to modern gymnastics. Jahn invented the side bar, horizontal bar, parallel bars, balance beam, and jumping events that still are practiced today, and by 1811 these events had come far enough along to act as selling points to a new school he opened that year.

Gymnastics clubs soon followed all over Europe, with participation in the events spreading like wildfire. The sport would find its way to the United States by the mid-1800s, when an American professor named Dr. Dudley Allen Sargent introduced it to myriad universities all over the country right around the time of the American Civil War.

THE OLYMPICS

The Fédération Internationale de Gymnastique (FIG), or in English, the International Gymnastics Federation, formed in 1881 and was followed by the first "modern" Olympic Games in 1896. The earliest events were not exactly like they are today; synchronized **calisthenics**, a sort of team aerobics event, served as the basis for gymnastic events in the Olympic Games then, while rope climbing, high jumping, running, and ladder climbing also appeared in some of those early games. Women were not even allowed to participate in Olympic gymnastics events until 1928.

The German team competes on the parallel bars at the first modern Olympic Games in 1896.

It was not until 1954 that the apparatus and events for gymnastic events in national and international competitions were completely standardized, but with professional sports growing increasingly popular and media coverage of events allowing for more widespread access—and, therefore, fandom of the Olympic Games—it was time to nail down an official, modernized version of the sport.

Balance beam is one of the events in a modern women's gymnastics competition.

STANDARDIZING THE SPORT

The results of that standardization included many important decisions. There would, for example, be both individual and team events for both men and women, and the floor, horizontal (high) bar, parallel bars, still rings, pommel horse, and vault were chosen as the men's events that would appear in the Olympics. For the women, they would compete in the floor exercise and the vault, along with the balance beam and uneven bars. A 10-point scoring system also was agreed to at that time.

It would not be long before gymnastics began to look a lot like the sport it is today. In 1962, rhythmic gymnastics was recognized by FIG as a legal gymnastics competition, and by the 1980s it, too, grew into a popular event at the Olympic Games. Trampoline, the last of the modern gymnastic events to earn medal status at the Olympics, was added in 2000, although further expansion of the sport always is possible.

Gymnastics is one of the oldest sports in the world, and its colorful history is a big part of what makes it such a respected and influential part of the modern Olympic canon. From the Ancient Greeks to 21st-century Olympic competitions, gymnastics remains among the best displays of grace, strength, and fitness in the world. As long as an appreciation for these things exists, so too will the sport of gymnastics.

Gymnastics room in the National Gymnastics Hall in Milwaukee, ca. 1900

 Text-Dependent Questions:

1. What is the Greek literal meaning of the word "gymnastics"?

2. Who is credited with developing the first complete course book for gymnastics?

3. In what year did the apparatus and events for gymnastic events in national and international competitions become completely standardized?

 Research Project:

Find out more about the "Grandfather of Gymnastics" through online research and books available at your local library. Next, make a list of those individuals credited with creating others sports such as football, baseball, and so on. Compare the efforts these individuals put forth to bring their respective sports to the public. What kind of pushback did they get? In your opinion, what personality traits are vital to take on these kinds of missions to create a new sport?

The original vaulting horse, seen here in 1959, caused serious injuries, and has been replaced by the vaulting table.

Words to Understand:

fluidity: the physical property of a substance that enables it to flow

apparatuses: a set of materials or equipment designed for a particular use

pommel horse: a large piece of equipment used in gymnastics that is like a very thick bench with two handles on top

CHAPTER 3

THE EVOLUTION OF EVENTS AND SCORING

In the thousands of years before gymnastics was an Olympic event, the Greeks and Romans considered those activities to be focused more toward combat training than anything competitive or with an emphasis on **fluidity** and grace. In the decades leading up to the first "modern" Olympic Games in 1896, as schools focused more on physical education and an actual sport of gymnastics started to form, the sport evolved tremendously. More than a century later, it is still evolving.

EARLY EVENTS

Today's gymnastics events took time to develop, not only in fine-tuning some of the **apparatuses**, rules, and judging criteria but also to determine what, exactly, gymnastics was going to encompass as a sport. It is, after all, a relatively focused discipline now, but it was not always that way.

In fact, as the Olympics grew in popularity between 1896 and 1924, a period in which the games were played only by men, a number of activities fell under the umbrella of "gymnastics" that no longer are considered as such. For example, early gymnasts were tasked with club swinging and rock lifting as part of their repertoire, and in some cases swimming even fell into this same category.

THE MODERN SPORT

Eventually, these early, primitive versions of gymnastics worked themselves out, with swimming now a sport all on its own and hammer throw or discus events in track and field closely resembling club swinging. By the 1950s there existed a standard competition for men and women all over the world, which looks very much today like it did then, with six events in the men's competition (vault, floor, parallel bars, horizontal bar, still rings, and pommel horse) and four for the women's competition (vault, balance beam, floor, and uneven bars).

This is not to say that there have not been changes in these activities over the course of the last 60 years. The vault event, for example, no longer uses the first apparatus that served as the event's single piece of equipment for more than 100 years. Due to a number of serious injuries stemming from the utilization of the first vaulting horse (essentially a pommel horse without handles), the apparatus was changed to what today is known as the vaulting table. It is flatter, larger, and more cushioned than the original version and thus far has proven a much safer option than the classic vaulting horse.

2015 European Artistic Gymnastics Championships vault

APPARATUS ADJUSTMENTS

The **pommel horse** also has undergone massive changes since its invention. With origins in combat training, the pommel horse is named the way it is because early versions of this exercise were literally about mounting and dismounting an actual horse with as much skill and grace as possible. It is such an old tool that Alexander the Great may even have used one to practice his mounting and dismounting skills. Today, however, these apparatuses do not look equine at all as they are covered with leather over foam-rubber padding for safety purposes.

The uneven bars also have undergone plenty of changes over the years as the event started by setting two men's parallel bars at different heights and performing routines not entirely unlike those carried out on the parallel bars—but certainly not as challenging as those elite gymnasts practice today. In the 1970s, manufacturers of gymnastic equipment started to develop unique, adjustable uneven bars that could be tethered to the ground with tension cables, improving the safety of the equipment and allowing for more adventurous movement from one bar to the next.

Uneven bars

SCORING CHANGES

Even the scoring of gymnastic competitions and events has undergone some changes over the years, the most controversial of which was the 2006 overhaul of the Code of Points, the rulebook defining the scoring system for gymnastics. In the 2004 Summer Olympics in Athens, Greece, there were a number of complaints about how certain events were scored, which inspired change in the sport's scoring system.

While still judged on a 10-point scale, as they have been since the 1920s, the new system of scoring changes how those points are compiled. Before 2006, gymnasts were given a start value based on routine difficulty with deductions taken from that score during the routine as needed. Now there are two scores—one for difficulty and another for execution—with the emphasis falling on artistry and overall value of performance more than difficulty.

Because these changes are both relatively new and a bit confusing to casual fans, some purists dislike them. Preferences aside, the truth is that the sport never will stop evolving as technology, safety, and the boundary pushing of the athletes dictate. As long as it continues to change for the better, artistic gymnastics very likely will long remain one of the most popular Olympic sports around the world.

The judges team during 32nd Rhythmic Gymnastics World Championship

Text-Dependent Questions:

1. How many events make up the men's competition? Is it the same for women?

2. Due to a number of serious injuries stemming from the utilization of the first vaulting horse, the apparatus was changed to what today is known as the vaulting table. Explain how the two apparatuses are different.

3. In what year was the Code of Points overhauled?

Research Project:

Visit some online forums in which gymnastic fans, athletes, and coaches are discussing changes to the scoring system and how this will play a role in the 2016 Olympic Games. What are people saying?

Team Italy performs a routine with balls and ribbons during the Rhythmic Gymnastics World Championships.

Words to Understand:

disciplines: activities, exercises, or regimens that develop or improve a skill; training

subjectively: modified or affected by personal views, experiences, or backgrounds

iterations: different forms or versions of something

CHAPTER 4

ARTISTIC, RHYTHMIC, AND OTHER GYMNASTICS DISCIPLINES

While the majority of the most famous gymnasts have participated in artistic gymnastics events, and American youths most often participate in that brand of the sport, the other variations of gymnastics have grown in the 21st century, even at Olympic competitions. Other important **disciplines** include rhythmic gymnastics, trampoline, power tumbling, aerobic gymnastics, and acrobatic gymnastics, although there are even more disciplines that exist today across the globe.

ARTISTIC GYMNASTICS

When tickets go on sale for the Summer Olympics, artistic gymnastics events almost always are the ones to sell out first. There are both individual and team titles for both men's and women's gymnastics, including vault, uneven bars, floor exercise, and balance beam for female competitors and vault, parallel bars, floor exercise, still rings, pommel horse, and horizontal bar for the men. Team events consist of five athletes, four of which compete in preliminaries and three of which compete in finals. Medals are doled out based on the total team score. For individuals, awards are given for each event, whereas an all-around medal also is awarded for the gymnast who scores the highest composite score across all events.

Gymnast performing with clubs

Gymnast performing with hoop

Gymnast performing with ribbon

RHYTHMIC GYMNASTICS

Another form of Olympic gymnastics is the rhythmic discipline, which currently is limited only to female athletes, at least in terms of international competitions, and includes events in rope, hoop, ball, clubs, and ribbon. Like artistic gymnastics, these events reward flexibility and grace, although these more fluid exhibitions typically lose some of the power and strength observed in many of the artistic gymnastics events. With an apparent basis in dance, ballet specifically, these routines showcase a very different set of skills, but the gymnastic element is still evident thanks to the inclusion of flips and tumbles. The 30-point scoring scale is different from the 10-point scale used in artistic gymnastics, but both disciplines look at both difficulty and mastery in awarding those scores.

TRAMPOLINE

Synchronized trampoline

Since being added to the Olympic slate in 2000, trampoline already has garnered significant interest from fans of the sport. Both men and women compete in this event, performed on a double mini trampoline, although there also is a synchronized trampoline event performed in some non-Olympic events by partners on two adjacent trampolines. The individual events are judged **subjectively** on a 10-point scale, with both difficulty and mastery factoring into the final number, although the essential part of the routine is a series of 10 jumps during which an aerial skill is performed during each bound.

POWER TUMBLING

Tumblers compete on a springy runway, during which time they are required to complete a number of flips and twists on each pass. Athletes are judged similarly to how they are judged in trampoline events, but unlike trampoline this is not an Olympic sport, although it is run at the Junior Olympics program in the United States.

AEROBIC GYMNASTICS

While many other gymnastics events are meant to show mastery over certain skills pertaining to agility and grace, aerobic gymnastics focuses more on strength and aerobic fitness, something that is evident through the performance of 60- to 90-second routines that require quite a bit of serious cardio exercise. These routines can be performed by individuals or groups of up to six people and are not currently under consideration for Olympic inclusion.

ACROBATIC GYMNASTICS

Whatever skills a person may need to be a successful circus performer could just as well be applied to acrobatic gymnastics, known as "Acro" for short. While dancing and tumbling do come into play during these routines, which can be performed by groups of two, three, or four people, what differentiates this type of gymnastics from other disciplines is the use of heads, hands, and feet to put together some truly impressive configurations of human strength and flexibility. Acrobatic gymnasts aren't contortionists per set, but with their skill sets, they would be right at home at Barnum & Bailey. The big tent of the Olympics is not yet ready for these performers, however.

Acrobatic women's pair

OTHER DISCIPLINES

While the aforementioned types of gymnastics are the most popular and widespread **iterations** of the sport, there are a handful of other types that exist as well. One example is aesthetic group gymnastics, which is similar to rhythmic gymnastics in style but does not use any equipment and consists of much larger groups than is typical in the rhythmic discipline. TeamGym competitions, which feature floor, tumbling, and trampette routines, also are growing increasingly popular in Europe, and men's rhythmic gymnastics also exists in some parts of the world. None of these are Olympic events.

"Gymnastics" is a term as flexible as the athletes who perform them, proven by the myriad disciplines that exist in the world today. While artistic gymnastics may be the most popular, there's little question that all of the disciplines are challenging and beautiful in their own rights.

Text-Dependent Questions:

1. What year was trampoline added to the Olympic slate?

2. Describe what differentiates acrobatic gymnastics from the other disciplines.

3. What type of competition, featuring floor, tumbling, and trampette routines, is growing increasingly popular in Europe?

Research Project:

Learn more about the various disciplines of gymnastics that are less popular and sparingly televised compared to those in artistic gymnastics. Print photos of gymnasts competing in each discipline, and create a scrapbook.

Rhythmic gymnastics have been included in the Olympic Games since 1984.

Words to Understand:

aspirations: eager desires for personal advancement

mainstays: something or someone to which one looks for support

burgeoning: to become greater in extent, volume, amount, or number

CHAPTER 5

THE OLYMPICS AND MODERN GYMNASTICS

Knowing that gymnastics is one of the most popular Olympic events among fans, it probably should not come as much of a surprise that it also is one of the most popular sports in the country in terms of youth participation. According to USA Gymnastics, there were more than 5.2 million participants age six or older in the United States as of 2015, with more than 4,000 gymnastics clubs scattered about the country.

A DISCIPLINE FOR CHILDREN

Of those millions of young American gymnasts, many have the dream of one day competing in the Olympics, to say nothing of all the other young athletes worldwide with the same **aspirations**. China, for example, is infamous for putting children as young as four years old into rigorous gymnastics training, with sights set on the gold and a place in national and Olympic history.

The reason for that head start is because the age limit for making the Olympic gymnastics team is only 16, meaning the equivalent of high school sophomores are competing on the most prestigious stage in their sport at an age much younger than, say, American football players, who must play two years in college before getting drafted, or the NBA, which requires that its athletes be at least 19 years old.

Today, it's easy to speculate that gymnastics are so popular because its biggest Olympic stars are so young. America loves child prodigies, and for the last 40 years, that is exactly what most of the elite gymnasts have been.

Romanian gymnast Nadia Comăneci seen during her practice session for an appearance at the Hartford Civic Center.

THE OLDER DAYS

It wasn't always that way. In the 1950s and 1960s, the star of the female gymnastics world was a Russian gymnast named Larisa Latynina, still the most decorated female Olympian of all time, and she made her debut in her 20s. Her principal rival, Hungarian Agnes Keleti, started her own Olympic career in her early 30s. These were women with roots in the art of ballet, and it was their years of dancing experience that, at the time, qualified them for these events.

In 1972 in Munich, however, 17-year-old Olga Korbut of the Soviet Union burst onto the scene and took three gold medals ahead of many older, less exciting **mainstays**. Four years later, 14-year-old Romanian star Nadia Comăneci earned the sport's first perfect 10 scores, dethroning Korbut as the new darling of the event and helping set into motion a version of gymnastics where youth dominated.

YOUTH APPEAL

While the age limit eventually was changed to 16 in 1997, it hasn't changed the fact that television viewers, even casual fans of gymnastics, are enthralled by these youthful and energetic stars. In 2012, when the "Fierce Five" was fighting for all-around gold and Gabby Douglas was dominating the international competition, 29.6 million American viewers tuned in, putting up a 9.3 rating among adults 18 to 49 and doubling the number of viewers who tuned in for the same events in 2008.

Olympic gymnasts Kyla Ross, Aly Raisman, Jordyn Weiber, Gabby Douglas, and McKayla Maroney attend the 86th Annual Macy's Thanksgiving Day Parade on November 22, 2012, in NYC.

Part of the draw is that gymnastics events are as challenging as any that take place at an Olympic Games; almost everybody knows how to swim or run, but very few people have the skill to pull off multiple consecutive backflips or even get themselves up high enough to clear a vault. The fact that **burgeoning** adults not far removed from their youth are mastering these events makes them must-see TV, and knowing that they have devoted their entire childhoods to that mastery, despite the small odds of ever making an Olympic roster, makes the sport even more intriguing.

INCREASE BY REDUCTION

The sad news for some of these aspiring gymnasts is that it will prove even more challenging to make an Olympic gymnastics team in the very near future. In May of 2015, the International Gymnastics Federation approved a new format for the 2020 Summer Olympics in Tokyo that will cut the number of athletes on a gymnastics team from five to four.

The benefit to reducing team sizes is to give athletes from historically less powerful countries a better opportunity to qualify for the Olympic Games. There are great gymnasts in the world without a strong national team, and this change should help provide them with an increased chance to compete against the world's best.

GO FOR THE GOLD

Those who do finally reach the Olympics, no matter their ages, are given the opportunity of a lifetime, competing in front of millions of people all over the world as the culmination of a life's hard work. Some cultures accept nothing less than gold, but to earn any medal at that level is a massive accomplishment in artistic gymnastics, rhythmic gymnastics, and trampoline.

It is not an easy process. The odds of making the Olympics are right around 1 in 300,000. In comparison, Americans have a 1 in 190,000 chance of getting hit by a bolt of lightning in a given year. Even though it is a long shot, it is a dream that young athletes will never stop reaching to achieve.

Text-Dependent Questions:

1. What country is infamous for putting children as young as four years old into rigorous gymnastics training, with sights set on the gold and a place in national and Olympic history?

2. In what year did the age limit for Olympic gymnasts change to 16?

3. In May of 2015, the International Gymnastics Federation approved a new format for the 2020 Summer Olympics in Tokyo that will cut the number of athletes on a gymnastics team. How many gymnasts will now make up the team?

Research Project:

As discussed in this chapter, the minimum age for gymnasts competing in the Olympics has changed several times over the years. Examine the difference in historical age minimums in gymnastics versus four other popular sports. Create a chart to compare your findings. Next, have a friend or family member videotape you presenting your chart and explaining your research on age minimums. Don't just share the facts with your viewers; share your thoughts too on how age minimums are either good or bad for each of these sports.

Gabby Douglas

Words to Understand:

adoration: strong feelings of love or admiration

lauded: praised

linchpin: a person or thing that holds something together; the most important part of a complex situation or system

juggernaut: something that is extremely large and powerful and cannot be stopped

CHAPTER 6

MODERN-DAY STARS

The names that stick in the collective memories of the American public almost always are female competitors in women's artistic gymnastics, which should not come as too big a surprise when one considers that more than 70 percent of the participants in competitive gymnastics in the United States are, in fact, women. The odds simply are in favor of young women producing the majority of the biggest stars.

The 2012 Summer Olympics in London were no exception to this trend, with the "Fierce Five" winning the United States' second team gold in the history of the sport and riding that victory to massive public **adoration** and overwhelming popularity. However, the United States only recently began experiencing some dominance in the world of gymnastics, and it by no means has a stranglehold on the sport, especially in men's gymnastics.

Historically, European and Asian gymnasts have dominated the sport on the Olympic stage, but with the Americans steadily improving, there now are myriad diverse and talented young stars across all disciplines from many countries.

The five members of the gold medal winning U.S. women's gymnastics team from the 2012 Olympic Games visited President Barack Obama at the White House in November 2012.

Gabby Douglas

Simone Biles

Aliya Mustafina

WOMEN

The most recent of America's gymnastics sweethearts, Douglas was a key member of the aforementioned "Fierce Five" who won team gold at the 2012 Olympics. She also was the top athlete in the women's all-around competition that year, giving her the two most prestigious medals in gymnastics and making her the first woman of African descent to be named the Olympic all-around champion. She is about as decorated as gymnasts come.

Douglas's older sister was a cheerleader and had Gabby learning basic tumbling skills as early as age four. By age six, Douglas had started her formal training and would be named Virginia's 2004 Gymnastics State Champion at the tender age of eight. Eventually, she earned a spot on the 2011 World Championships team that would win team gold, and in the following year she would place first at the Olympic Trials on her way to those two gold medals in London. Douglas then won team gold and an individual all-around silver medal at the 2015 World Championships.

The all-around gold medal at those 2015 World Championships went to Douglas's teammate, Simone Biles. Whereas Douglas proved that gymnasts of African descent could see tremendous success on the biggest stage in the sport, up-and-comer Biles has continued that trend as the most **lauded** young gymnast in the world. While she was only 15 years old for the 2012 Summer Olympics, she has proven in the years since that she is every bit as talented as Douglas, if not more so.

Aliya Mustafina of Russia performs an exercise on the uneven bars in the final of the 5th European Championships in Artistic Gymnastics in Moscow, Russia, on April 20, 2013.

Biles's victory at the 2015 World Championships gave her gold in the all-around competition there for the third consecutive year. She also won the competition as the top all-around gymnast at the U.S. National Championships for three straight years and took top honors in balance beam in both 2014 and 2015. She already is the most decorated gymnast in the history of the World Championships, with 10 gold medals and 14 medals in total through 2015. Before it is all said and done, Biles could end up being even more celebrated than Douglas.

Biles's biggest competition may not be Douglas but more likely Russia's Aliya Mustafina. The daughter of an Olympic Greco-Roman wrestling bronze medalist, Mustafina was born with the fire of competition in her blood. As the **linchpin** for the talented Russian artistic gymnastics team, Mustafina won the bronze in the all-around at the 2012 Olympics and led her Russian teammates to a team silver, a tremendous accomplishment against the bevy of talent in those Olympics and even more impressive considering Mustafina was coming off a torn ACL in April of 2011.

Prior to the London Olympics, Mustafina won two gold medals at the 2010 World Championships, including one for the all-around. After London, she won gold on the balance beam at the 2013 World Championships. Through 2015, Mustafina had collected 11 World Championship medals and four Olympic medals. She missed the 2015 World Championships with a back injury, but when healthy, she is a dominant force in the sport.

Nadia Comăneci and her incredible legacy have been a dominant force in gymnastics for decades. As a Romanian artistic gymnastics prodigy, Larisa Lordache never was going to escape comparisons to fellow Romanian legend Comăneci, the first gymnast to score a perfect 10 in the sport's history. Lordache, however, has done plenty to make a big name for herself, despite her small stature. At 4'11" (1.5 m) she is about as sprightly as they come in Olympic gymnastics, and her skills in floor exercise are respected across the gymnastics community. She was the primary reason the Romanian team won the team bronze medal in London, and since then Iordache has won four World Championship medals, including all-around silver in 2014 and bronze in 2015.

Rhythmic gymnastics consists of an entirely different set of events from the artistic events that draw such big television ratings, but as Russia's Yana Kudryavtseva has proven, dominance in those exercises are no less impressive than in other events. Without question, Kudryavtseva is the Michael Jordan of rhythmic gymnastics, having won three consecutive all-around gold medals at the World Championships plus eight more individual gold medals and two team gold medals since 2013. There is little doubt that the so-called Crystal Statuette is the world's best at rhythmic gymnastics.

Nadia Comăneci

Yana Kudryavtseva

MEN

Widely considered to be the most gifted male gymnast alive, Kōhei Uchimura remains a **juggernaut** in the sport well into his 20s, At the 2015 World Championships, at age 26, he earned the gold medal in the all-around, the sixth time he has done that since 2009. In fact, during that span he won 15 individual medals and 4 team medals, 10 of which were gold. Uchimura won every all-around World Championship and Olympic gold medal between 2009 and 2015 (that is six consecutive World Championships plus the 2012 Olympics). He is literally the gold standard in men's gymnastics and has been the most recognizable man in the sport for nearly a decade.

Arguably the most talented and recognizable athlete in U.S. men's gymnastics, Californian Sam Mikulak is a 2012 Summer Olympics veteran. His professional career started while attending college at the University of Michigan, during which time he also competed in national and international gymnastics competitions, including the 2012 Olympics. He injured himself during the Olympic Trials, however, and was kept out of most events while there. In 2013, he finished fourth in the high bar and sixth in all-around at the 2013 World Artistic Gymnastics Championships and helped lead the U.S. team that won bronze at the 2014 Worlds competition. As the three-time defending U.S. Nationals champion, and the 2015 Pan American Games all-around champion, Mikulak is the best American medal hope in any men's competition.

Kōhei Uchimura

Sam Mikulak

Max Whitlock

Mikulak's teammate, Donnell Whittenburg, is close on his heels from a competitive standpoint. An absolute mountain of a man, Whittenburg is the sort of physical specimen that drops jaws at the sight of his powerful form. A good physique is far from his only talent, however, as this vault specialist is a rising star in men's gymnastics.

Growing up, Whittenburg spent his time performing what he called "backyard gymnastics," so his mother found him a gym to burn off his youthful energy and keep him from breaking his neck without proper safety equipment and coaching. It did not take long for the coaches at his gym to recognize his innate talent, and he was added to his first gymnastics team practically right away. Whittenburg placed third in vault at the 2015 World Championships, placed eighth in the all-around, and was a member of the third-place U.S. men's team at the 2014 World Championships as well.

Great Britain isn't typically considered a gymnastics powerhouse, but at the 2014 World Championships, the men's gymnastics team that finished one spot ahead of Whittenburg and the Americans followed up with another second-place finish in 2015. All it took to make the difference was one transcendent athlete to turn the tide for the program and earn them widespread respectability. Max Whitlock was that athlete for the Great Britain team. In 2012, he led his squad to a bronze medal in front of the home fans at the London Olympics and won another bronze in pommel horse in the process. It was the first time in more than 100 years that a British men's team medaled at all. He also has a gold medal in three of the last four European Championships, including a team gold in 2012 and a gold medal in pommel horse at the 2015 World Championships in Glasgow, Scotland.

While pommel horse is Whitlock's strength, when it comes to parallel bars, there might not be a more talented gymnast alive than Ukraine's Oleg Vernyayev, who won the gold in that event at the World Championships in 2014 and the silver in 2015. While at 18 years old he didn't walk away with any medals at the 2012 London Olympics, he and his Ukrainian team finished fourth overall by a mere 0.2 points, and even that was controversial following an appeal on scoring that knocked Ukraine out of the medals. Vernyayev now has the strength and maturity to make more of an impact at future Olympic Games, and based on his gold medal at the 2015 European Games and fourth-place finish in the 2015 World Championships all-around, there is every reason to believe that the Ukrainian will be vying for gold medals in every competition he enters.

Max Whitlock of Great Britain performs an exercise on the pommel horse.

Text-Dependent Questions:

1. Who was the first woman of African descent to be named the Olympic all-around champion in 2012?

2. Name the Russian gymnast who is the Michael Jordan of rhythmic gymnastics, having won three consecutive all-around gold medals at the World Championships plus eight more individual gold medals and two team gold medals since 2013.

3. In 2012, which gymnast led his squad to a bronze medal in front of his home fans at the London Olympics, leading to the first time in more than 100 years that a British men's team medaled at all?

Research Project:

Pick a top gymnast from each of four countries of your choice. Do some online research to learn more about them and their careers. Watch videos of them competing at various meets. How old were they when they started? What kinds of sacrifices have they made to be where they are today? Share your findings.

SHANNON MILLER

YELENA SHUSHUNOVA

OLGA KORBUT

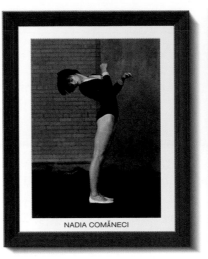

NADIA COMĂNECI

VĚRA ČÁSLAVSKÁ

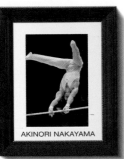

AKINORI NAKAYAMA

LUDMILLA TOURISCHEVA

LARISA LATYNINA   NIKOLAI ANDRIANOV   NELLIE KIM

DMITRY BILOZERCHEV

TAKASHI ONO

BORIS SHAKHLIN

The strength, agility and endurance of world class gymnasts is astounding to the average person. The very best of these elite athletes also add the elements of artistry and grace, giving the sport an aesthetic quality unlike any other. The sport is governed internationally by the Fédération Internationale de Gymnastique (FIG), which is based in Switzerland. Known in English as the International Gymnastics Federation, FIG sets the rules that determine how gymnastics competitions are judged. Learn more by scanning the QR code on this page.

CHAPTER 7

GYMNASTICS' GREATEST ATHLETES

Like all sports, gymnastics has changed quite a bit over the years, particularly in the way that its athletes are judged. As gymnasts have grown more adept at mastering ever-more sophisticated routines, the way experts define "greatness" changes, but with so many different events in the sport, it can be quite challenging to compare apples to oranges (or, in this case, vault specialists to floor routine pros).

When it comes to Olympic greatness, however, there are a few simple ways to determine which men and women were the best ever—really high scores and loads of gold medals. Even that isn't easy to quantify as the scoring system has changed monumentally over time, particularly in the last decade or so. The most recent alteration came in 2006 when the Code of Points rule book was completely reconfigured to create a more objective judging system that rewarded athletes for completing the right number and sequence of challenging tasks rather than allowing judges to throw up more subjective scores.

It used to be that the perfect 10 was the ultimate symbol of greatness in gymnastics, and in fact, several of the most cherished athletes in the sport are so beloved because they achieved that mythical score, which once was considered to be impossible.

The new Code of Points allows scores to end up much higher than 10, and every event has a different possible "perfect" score. That doesn't mean it is any easier to identify greatness than it was before 2006; it just means that today, a pile of Olympic medals is a much easier way to pick out the top gymnasts than a confusing score arrived upon by means not understood by casual fans.

Whatever the criteria, there have been a number of amazing athletes in the history of gymnastics, and the following are the best of them:

MALE ATHLETES

Japan's Akinori Nakayama is one of only two gymnasts to earn gold in the Olympic rings event twice; Akinori also was part of two consecutive Olympic gold medal teams in 1968 and

1972. He also owns gold medals in parallel bars and horizontal bar as well as consecutive silver medals in the floor exercise.

While repeating Olympic success is impressive, dominating a single games has its cachet as well. In the 1980 Moscow Olympics, the former Soviet Union's Alexander Dityatin pulled in a record eight medals, which has been tied in the years since but has not been surpassed. Seven of those were individual medals, another record that also held until American swimmer Michael Phelps ultimately exceeded it.

When Phelps broke the record for most all-time medals in 2008, the former Soviet Union's Nikolai Andrianov was the man whose record fell. He finished his career with 15 of them, including 7 gold medals, earned in the team, all-around, floor, rings, and vault events from 1972 to 1980.

Dmitry Bilozerchev of the Soviet Union was also a multi-event specialist. Bilozerchev was the epitome of technique, form, and style in his time, which is why he won two world all-around titles and three Olympic gold medals at the 1988 Games in Seoul. Even after breaking his leg in more than 40 places in a 1985 car crash, he regained his title at the World Championships in 1987.

Akinori Nakayama

Dmitry Bilozerchev

The Ukraine's Viktor Chukarin also has a story of perseverance. He was wounded in combat fighting the Nazis for the Soviet army in World War II. After being shot, he spent more than three years as a prisoner of war and weighed just 88 pounds when he was rescued in 1945. Chukarin was 30 years old before he made it to his first Olympics at Helsinki in 1952. There, he won four gold medals including the all-around title. He won three gold medals at the 1954 World Championships, again including the all-around title. At 34, Chukarin won three more golds at the 1956 Olympic Games in Melbourne, Australia.

Few won more medals than Alexander Nemov, one of the most decorated gymnasts, male or female, in the history of the sport. Nemov was a showman in his time, competing in three different Olympic Games (1996, 2000, and 2004) and performing jaw-dropping, ultra-complicated moves in each of them. The 2000 Olympic all-around champion, he remains one of Russia's most beloved athletes.

As revered as Nemov is in Russia, it is hard to match the adoration the Japanese people have for Sawao Kato. Between 1968 and 1976, he won a whopping 12 Olympic medals, 8 of which were gold, and he helped an incredibly strong Japan team dominate the 1972 Olympics, where only 6 of 21 medals went to other countries. Kato is 1 of only 10 Olympic athletes to have won more than 8 gold medals in a career.

Alexander Nemov

Sawao Kato

Eight is the magic number in men's gymnastics. Just ask Vitaly Scherbo of Belarus, who holds the record as the only gymnast ever to win all eight world events over the course of his career. Scherbo dominated the 1992 Barcelona Olympics by taking gold medals in six of the eight events there, including team, all-around, vault, rings, pommel horse, and parallel bars.

The former Soviet Union's Boris Shakhlin retired with an impressive record of his own. He is the one-time world record holder for most Olympic medals, which was set at 13 when he won four medals at the 1964 Tokyo Games. Shakhlin remained a strong competitor well into his 30s and only retired because he had a heart attack at age 35. Had he remained healthy, he may have continued racking up medals to add to his record.

Takashi Ono of Japan may have won several more medals in his Olympic career were it not for the dominance of Shakhlin. Ono is that rare gymnast with gold medals in three consecutive Olympic Games, including one in 1954, three in 1960, and one in 1964. He also has four silver and four bronze medals from that era as well.

Boris Shakhlin

Takashi Ono

FEMALE ATHLETES

One of only two female gymnasts in history to take home all-around gold in two consecutive Olympics, the spirited Věra Čáslavská easily is the former Czechoslovakia's most decorated gymnast. Her seven Olympic gold medals in individual events between the 1964 Tokyo Olympics and 1968 Mexico City Olympics remains a record among female gymnasts.

Nadia Comăneci of Romania set the most famous record in the sport's history at the 1976 games in Montréal, Canada. Not only did she receive the first-ever perfect 10 score in Olympic gymnastics history, but she did so at age 14. She won three Olympic gold medals that year and then another two in 1980. She remains one of the most recognizable names in the sport and is credited with turning the sport onto its head in the 1970s at an age when most girls are just starting high school.

Comăneci's main competition at the Montréal Games was the former Soviet Union's Nellie Kim. Kim, whose father is of Korean descent, won gold in the vault and floor exercise, whereas Comăneci won the beam and uneven bars to edge Kim for the all-around title. Kim would go on to win the all-around gold at the 1979 World Championships. She won five Olympic and five World Championship gold medals in her career.

Věra Čáslavská

Nadia Comăneci

Nellie Kim

Olympic Stadium in Montréal, Canada

Winning medals defined the career of Russia's Svetlana Khorkina. As one of the most popular and talented gymnasts in an era when television ratings for the sport were on the rise, Khorkina made a tremendous impact both in Russia and the rest of the world by winning medals at three consecutive Olympics between 1996 and 2004. She was the first gymnast ever to win the world all-around title three consecutive times and finished her career with seven Olympic medals and a whopping 20 more in various World Championships. Olympic and World Championship all-around gold medals eluded Khorkina in her career.

Svetlana Khorkina

The closest Khorkina came to winning the Olympic team gold was in Atlanta in 1996, where she lost to a U.S. team led by Oklahoma native Shannon Miller. Miller had won five medals at the 1992 Games in Barcelona, Spain, but no individual gold medals and just a bronze in the team event. Having won back-to-back World Championship all-around titles in 1993 and 1994, Miller was one of the favorites to shine in Atlanta. She did not disappoint, winning the balance beam gold and leading her "Magnificent Seven" American teammates to the country's first-ever women's team gold.

In 1972, Olga Korbut of the former Soviet Union pulled off some first-ever, never-before-seen balance beam routines that showed more of a leaning toward acrobatics than artistry, and that rejuvenated gymnastics and helped grow the sport with youths worldwide. Korbut won gold in both the beam and floor exercise events. She battled some injuries at the 1976 Olympics, but those 1972 games were incredible both for her daring and for the future of the events she helped to redefine.

Shannon Miller

Outshined in some ways by Korbut, her pioneering teammate in the 1972 Munich Olympics, Ludmilla Tourischeva still was the real force in the sport that year. She won medals in all four events to capture both the team and individual all-around gold medals. Those medals were sandwiched by team gold at both the 1968 and 1976 Olympics, allowing her to retire with nine total Olympic medals over the course of 12 years mastering the sport.

One of the original pioneers of the modern version of the sport, Larisa Latynina won a record 18 Olympic medals, including 9 of them between 1956 and 1964, 9 of them gold. She won back-to-back Olympic all-around titles representing the former Soviet Union in 1956 and 1960. At 21 years old the year of her Olympic debut, Latynina was older than modern female gymnasts tend to be, but that didn't make her any less dominant in her era.

The best way for an athlete to prove she is one of the best in her craft in a given year is to dominate every event, which Daniela Silivaş did by medaling in every single event at the 1988 Olympics. She lost top all-around honors by a fraction of a point to the former Soviet Union's Yelena Shushanova but proved through her medals and her record seven perfect 10 scores that year that she really was the most dominant all-around gymnast in that particular Olympic Games.

Losing to Shushanova was nothing to be ashamed of for Silivaş. After all, that was often the result for most of the Russian's competitors in the mid-1980s. Aside from her Olympic all-around title at Seoul in 1988, Shushanova also led the Soviets to team gold. In the run-up to the 1988 Olympics, Shushanova won the European and the all-around World Championships in 1985. She retired after the Seoul Olympics with 15 Olympic and World Championship medals won over a four-year span.

Larisa Latynina

Ludmilla Tourischeva

Career Snapshots

Men

VIKTOR CHUKARIN 1946–1956

7 Olympic Gold Medals
3 World Championship Gold Medals
3 Major all-around titles

NIKOLAI ANDRIANOV 1971–1980

7 Olympic Gold Medals
4 World Championship Gold Medals
2 Major all-around titles

TAKASHI ONO 1956–1964

5 Olympic Gold Medals
2 World Championship Gold Medals
0 Major all-around titles

ALEXANDER DITYATIN 1975–1981

3 Olympic Gold Medals
7 World Championship Gold Medals
2 Major all-around titles

BORIS SHAKHLIN 1955–1966

7 Olympic Gold Medals
6 World Championship Gold Medals
2 Major all-around titles

DMITRY BILOZERCHEV 1983–1987

3 Olympic Gold Medals
8 World Championship Gold Medals
2 Major all-around titles

AKINORI NAKAYAMA 1966–1972

6 Olympic Gold Medals
7 World Championship Gold Medals
0 Major all-around titles

VITALY SCHERBO 1991–1996

6 Olympic Gold Medals
12 World Championship Gold Medals
2 Major all-around titles

SAWAO KATO 1968–1974

8 Olympic Gold Medals
1 World Championship Gold Medals
1 Major all-around title

ALEXEI NEMOV 1994–2003

4 Olympic Gold Medals
5 World Championship Gold Medals
1 Major all-around title

Women

LARISA LATYNINA 1954–1965

9 Olympic Gold Medals
9 World Championship Gold Medals
4 Major all-around titles

NADIA COMĂNECI 1975–1981

5 Olympic Gold Medals
2 World Championship Gold Medals
1 Major all-around title

VĚRA ČÁSLAVSKÁ 1958–1968

7 Olympic Gold Medals
4 World Championship Gold Medals
3 Major all-around titles

YELENA SHUSHUNOVA 1984–1988

2 Olympic Gold Medals
5 World Championship Gold Medals
2 Major all-around titles

LUDMILLA TOURISCHEVA 1968–1976

4 Olympic Gold Medals
7 World Championship Gold Medals
3 Major all-around titles

DANIELA SILIVAȘ 1985–1989

3 Olympic Gold Medals
7 World Championship Gold Medals
0 Major all-around titles

OLGA KORBUT 1972–1977

4 Olympic Gold Medals
2 World Championship Gold Medals
0 Major all-around titles

SHANNON MILLER 1991–2000

2 Olympic Gold Medals
5 World Championship Gold Medals
2 Major all-around titles

NELLIE KIM 1974–1980

5 Olympic Gold Medals
5 World Championship Gold Medals
1 Major all-around titles

SVETLANA KHORKINA 1994–2004

2 Olympic Gold Medals
9 World Championship Gold Medals
3 Major all-around titles

A West Virginia University gymnast competes on the vault during a dual meet.

Words to Understand:

empirical: provable or verifiable by experience or experiment

aficionados: ardent devotees, fans, or enthusiasts

CHAPTER 8

THE FUTURE OF GYMNASTICS

The perfect 10 score dramatically boosted the popularity of gymnastics, but it is now gone thanks to scoring controversies in the 2004 Summer Olympics. Now there is a complicated system with no scoring ceiling. The controversies and subsequent changes were unexpected and illustrate how difficult it is to predict the future of gymnastics. Gymnastics' future often has been dictated by efforts to resolve problems.

MORE DIFFICULT ROUTINES

The previous scoring system resulted in too many razor-thin differences between competitors. Close contests are exciting for fans, but scores were based in large part on opinions and interpretation rather than **empirical** measures. Consequently, judges made decisions that angered people. A dispute about whether American Paul Hamm or South Korean Yang Tae Young won the gold medal in the men's all-around competition at the 2004 Olympics was decided by a court. Hamm won.

The new system went into effect in 2006, replacing a system that existed for about 80 years. Essentially, FIG created a two-part system. In the first part, gymnasts start with zero points, and their score improves whenever they execute a complicated maneuver. They are awarded more points for more difficult moves. The second part is like the old system. It starts at 10 and deducts for mistakes. The new system encourages gymnasts to try more challenging, athletic, and daring moves—and will spur more complicated routines in the future.

OLDER GYMNASTS

Another rules change that was made to resolve problems was the decision to raise the minimum age for competing in international events against adults. As gymnastics became more popular in the 1970s, the average age of female gymnasts declined significantly. Many people noticed many younger gymnasts were having physical, mental, and emotional problems. Some seemed unnaturally thin. Others had problems handling stress.

The minimum age for "senior" gymnasts was raised from 14 to 15 in 1982 and to 16 in 1997. Over the years, some of the world's best gymnasts competed in "junior" events and excelled in senior events shortly after turning 15 or 16. In recent years, though, there has been more

A gymnast performs in the floor exercise during the men's competition at the VISA Nationals Gymnastics Championships in Hartford, CT.

Under a new scoring system, athletes like this pommel horse competitor are awarded points for attempting more difficult maneuvers.

evidence that intense physical activity before puberty slows girls' physical development. In the future, further medical findings may lead to girls becoming involved actively in gymnastics at a later age, meaning the top gymnasts will be older.

SAFETY CHANGES

A 2008 *Time* magazine article titled "Making Gymnastics Safer for Kids" reported that gymnasts are just as likely to be hurt as basketball, hockey, and soccer players, and the sport has one of female sports' highest injury rates.

Injury rates, though, have fallen sharply since 1990 because of better safety measures and equipment, including longer and wider pommel horses and better, padded safety mats. Gymnastics **aficionados** should expect coaches in the future to be better trained in teaching gymnasts how to avoid injuries, how to be better conditioned, and when to exercise and rest. Further improvements in equipment safety are also likely.

INCREASING NUMBER OF PARTICIPANTS

Several studies have shown a steady decrease in youth sports participation in this century. The number of 6- to 12-year-olds in the United States who played softball, football, baseball, soccer, and basketball fell 31.3, 28.6, 13.7, 10.7, and 3.9 percent, respectively, from 2008 to 2013.

The number of Americans at least six years old participating in gymnastics soared, though, from 3.63 million in 2006 to 5.4 million in 2012. The future looks bright, partly because data shows American children are more individualistic than kids of previous generations.

INCREASING NUMBER OF SPECTATORS

A 2015 report by Sports Media Watch said that 2.4 million people watched the women's competition at the USA Gymnastics Championships on a Saturday night, while a nationally broadcast Major League Baseball game that night had 239,000 viewers.

Trends might be more important than numbers. The gymnastics telecast was up 23 percent in ratings over the 2014 telecast, while baseball's numbers are declining. In the future, gymnastics aficionados can expect television ratings to be very high if American women do well.

MORE COMPETITIVE NATIONS

In 2015, the International Federation of Gymnastics reduced the number of members of each Olympic team from five to four, effective in 2020. Teams had seven members in 1996, six in 2000, and five in 2012. In 2012, 98 male and 98 female gymnasts participated in the Olympics. Sixty from each gender were from the 12 nations that qualified for the team competition. The change means that the number of gymnasts from countries traditionally weaker in gymnastics could increase from 38 to 50 per gender. In addition, Olympic rules that went into effect in 2012 permit only two gymnasts per nation to qualify for individual event finals. In 2012, American Jordyn Weiber was fourth in the all-around preliminaries but wasn't in the finals because Americans finished second and third.

Olympic Stadium, 2012 Summer Olympics,
London, United Kingdom

Olympic Stadium, 2008 Summer Olympics,
Beijing, China

Olympic Stadium, 2004 Summer Olympics,
Athens, Greece

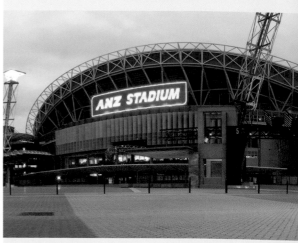

Olympic Stadium, 2000 Summer Olympics,
Sydney, Australia

Olympic Stadium, 1988 Summer Olympics,
Seoul, South Korea

Olympic Stadium, 1984 Summer Olympics
Los Angeles, United States

These changes mean that nations with more world-class gymnasts will have less of an edge. Gymnastics' future also could include more gymnasts competing for countries they have never lived in. Alaina Kwan and Kylie Dickson competed for Belarus in the 2015 world championships after finishing 9th and 11th in the U.S. Championships, although neither ever visited Belarus.

FUTURE STARS

LAURIE HERNANDEZ

The 2015 U.S. national all-around junior champion is New Jersey's Laurie Hernandez. Born in 2000, her win in 2015 was an improvement over a second-place finish in 2013. Hernandez missed the 2014 Nationals due to injury but won every meet she entered in 2014 and 2015. She was eligible to compete in the 2016 Olympic Games in Rio de Janeiro, Brazil.

LAURA ZENG

The highest American finisher in the women's rhythmic gymnastics all-around competition at the 2012 Summer Olympics was 21st. Laura Zeng, who was born in 1999, finished eighth in the 2015 World Rhythmic Gymnastics Championships one month before her 16th birthday. No American has ever medaled at the World Championships, which was first held in 1963 and has been held annually or every other year since then.

Laurie Hernandez

Laura Zeng

Text-Dependent Questions:

1. The new scoring system went into effect in 2006, replacing a system that existed for how many years?

2. In recent years there has been more evidence that intense physical activity before puberty slows girls' physical development. As further medical findings come to light, how is this expected to affect the age at which girls may become involved actively in gymnastics?

3. Name one up-and-coming star in the gymnastics world.

Research Project:

Put your journalistic skills to the test! Find out if your local gymnastics schools are seeing an increase in the numbers of participants learning the sport. Ask to interview the owners, coaches, and some athletes, then write an article to support your findings. If your findings are newsworthy, maybe your school paper will publish your article. Or you can also ask if the gymnastics schools will publish it on their Web sites or social media sites!

GLOSSARY OF GYMNASTICS TERMS

alteration: a change, an adjustment.

collective: with all members of a group, done together.

compiled: collected and put together.

composite: put together from different parts.

controversial: causing disagreement.

debut: the first time someone does something in public.

dismount: to get off of or down from something.

enthralled: to hold attention by being very exciting or beautiful.

equivalent: equal, the same.

exuberance: large amounts of or intense energy or activity.

garnered: to earn, get, or receive.

intangible: not physical, not able to be touched.

ligaments: tissue in the body that holds bones together.

mastery: able to display great skill.

physique: the form or shape of a person's body.

poise: a confident, gracious manner.

preliminaries: an event before the main competition to determine which athletes are going to participate.

prestigious: highly regarded.

purist: someone who has clear ideas about what is right and often opposes change to tradition.

reconfigured: rearranged, reorganized.

rigorous: strict, demanding, detailed.

speculate: to guess, to predict based on little information.

sprightly: energetic, full of life.

stranglehold: a strong force that stops change or growth.

standardized: following the same rules, making things similar and consistent.

synchronized: happening the same way at the same time and at the same speed.

tethered: tied down.

transcendent: much better than expected or than others in the same group.

vying: trying very hard to win.

CHRONOLOGY

1758: German Johann Basedow, considered the first modern writer and teacher of organized gymnastics, makes gymnastics part of the educational curriculum at his school in Saxony.

1811: German Friedrich Jahn opens the first gymnastics club and goes on to invent the parallel bars, the rings, the balance beam, the horse, and the horizontal bar, which become standard equipment for the sport.

1881: FIG (Fédération Internationale de Gymnastique) is formed in Belgium in 1881 and pioneers international competitions.

1896: Gymnastics is a medal sport for men at the first modern Olympics in Athens.

1928: Women's gymnastics are added for the Summer Olympics in Amsterdam.

1934: The balance beam is first used in World Championship competition, measuring just 8 cm (3 inches) wide.

1952: Individual apparatus competition is added as medal events for women at the Summer Olympics in Helsinki.

1954: Gymnastics competitions are standardized to include six events for men and four for women. Scoring is also standardized with the 10 to 1 scoring system.

1956: The Soviet Union's Larisa Latynina wins the first of her record 14 individual Olympic medals. She also won three consecutive team gymnastics gold medals as Russian women's teams won every Olympics they competed in from 1952 to 1992.

1962: Rhythmic gymnastics are recognized as a sport by FIG.

1964: The first World Trampoline and Tumbling Championships are staged in London, England. Federations from 12 countries participate.

1970: The United States Gymnastics federation is formed.

1976: Nadia Comăneci from Romania gets the first perfect 10.0 score in a gymnastics event in the 1976 Summer Olympics in Montréal.

1981: Comăneci's coach Béla Károlyi and his wife Márta defect to the U.S., where he proceeds to coach Mary Lou Retton to the 1984 all-around Olympic gold medal. The couple had a great influence on U.S. gymnastics, also coaching gold medalists Kim Zmeskal, Dominique Moceanu, and Kerri Strug.

2000: Trampolining events are added at the 2000 Summer Olympics in Sydney.

2006: The 10 to 1 (perfect 10.0) scoring system is replaced by the Code of Points, a new scoring system designed to encourage more difficulty and promote objectivity.

Gymnastics Today: Legendary Romanian coaches Octavian Bellu and Mariana Bitang are coaxed out of retirement to lead the women's national team at an April 2016 test event to determine qualification for the 2016 Rio Olympics. The Romanian team failed to qualify for Rio after an embarrassing 13th place finish at the 2015 World Championships. Romania had not failed to qualify for the Olympics since 1972.

FURTHER READING

Lawrence, Blythe. *Great Moments in Olympic Gymnastics (Great Moments in Olympic Sports).* Edina, MN: Sportszone Publishers, 2014

Douglas, Gabrielle. *Raising the Bar.* Grand Rapids, MI: Zondervan, 2013

Stanley, Glen F., and Wesley, Ann. *Gymnastics: Girls Rocking It (Title IX Rocks!).* New York, NY: Rosen Publishing Group, 2016

INTERNET RESOURCES:

USA Gymnastics: https://usagym.org/pages/index.html

International Gymnastics Federation: http://www.fig-gymnastics.com/site/

Olympic.org: http://www.olympic.org/gymnastics-artistic

Rhythmic Gymnastics: http://www.olympic.org/gymnastics-rhythmic

VIDEO CREDITS:

Olga Korbut Charms the World (pg 8): https://www.youtube.com/watch?v=c2NGqIGFqeQ

Comăneci Is Perfect(pg 9): https://www.youtube.com/watch?v=Yi_5xbd5xdE

Fujimoto Fights the Pain (pg 10): https://www.youtube.com/watch?v=Gq-C5-vlim8

Retton Vaults to Fame (pg 11): https://www.youtube.com/watch?v=IX0HW1jnKYQ

Golden Men (pg 12): http://www.tubechop.com/watch/7756012

Rhythmic Perfection (pg 13): https://www.youtube.com/watch?v=o-P5zcTf5O4

Strug's Vault (pg 14): https://www.youtube.com/watch?v=7ZRYiOa5lM8

Hamming It Up (pg 15): http://www.tubechop.com/watch/7831326

QR CODES AND LINKS TO THIRD-PARTY CONTENT

You may gain access to certain third-party content ("Third-Party Sites") by scanning and using the QR Codes that appear in this publication (the "QR Codes"). We do not operate or control in any respect any information, products, or services on such Third-Party Sites linked to by us via the QR Codes included in this publication, and we assume no responsibility for any materials you may access using the QR Codes. Your use of the QR Codes may be subject to terms, limitations, or restrictions set forth in the applicable terms of use or otherwise established by the owners of the Third-Party Sites. Our linking to such Third-Party Sites via the QR Codes does not imply an endorsement or sponsorship of such Third-Party Sites, or the information, products, or services offered on or through the Third-Party Sites, nor does it imply an endorsement or sponsorship of this publication by the owners of such Third-Party Sites.

PICTURE CREDITS

Page: 3: Luigi Fardella/Shutterstock.com; 6: GeneralMills; MizMamie/youtube.com, U.S. Army photo by Sgt. Brandon D. Bolick/Released, 6, 44:Helga Esteb/Shutterstock.com, M.Stasy/Shutterstock.com, s_bukley/Shutterstock.com, Helga Esteb/ Shutterstock.com, 8: Olympics/youtube.com; 7: freelanceartist/Shutterstock.com; 8, 9, 11, 13: Olympics/youtube.com; 10: MizMamie/youtube.com; 12: westnyacktwins/youtube.com; 14: Team USA/youtube.com; 15: Jonah James/youtube. com; 16: Jastrow; 17: Acquired by Henry Walters, 1924; 18, 19, 20, 50, 52, 55: Public Domain; 18: De Visu/Shutterstock. com; 19: Kroon, Ron / Anefo; 21: tankist276 /Shutterstock.com; 22: Nationaal Archief, Den Haag; 23: fizkes/Shutterstock. com; 24: Pierre-Yves Beaudouin; 25: TwoWings; 26: katatonia82/Shutterstock.com; 27: Sergey Golotvin/Shutterstock.com; 28, 42, 43, 48, 56, 61, 70: Lilyana Vynogradova/Shutterstock.com; 29: Bauken77, LGEPR, cdephotos; 30: Trampqueen; 31: Poleydee; 32, 58: I T A L O /Shutterstock.com; 33: PhotoStock10/Shutterstock.com; 34: Luca Villanova/Shutterstock.com, Lucky Team Studio/Shutterstock.com; 35: Jiang Dao Hua/Shutterstock.com; 36, 50: Dave Gilbert; 37: lev radin/Shutterstock. com, Aspen Photo/Shutterstock.com; 38: ID1974/Shutterstock.com; 39: Gl0ck/Shutterstock.com; 40: s_bukley/Shutterstock. com; 41: Official White House Photo by Pete Souza; 42: Rena Schild/Shutterstock.com, Byarturo; 44: Cisco79; 45: Solodov Alexey/Shutterstock.com; 46: Rick McCharles, Joy VanBuhler, Anthony Berkeley; 49: Pol Hansen/Shutterstock.com; 50: Intel Free Press, Anefo / Croes, R.C, Post of Azerbaijan, 50, 51, 55: Kroon, Ron / Anefo, 50, 51: Anefo / Croes, R.C., Croes, Rob C. / Anefo, German Federal Archive, Vladimir Fedorenko; 52: JanSchroeder; 54: Galina Barskaya/Shutterstock.com; 56: Nizozemský archiv, Gabinho; 57: Antoine Mghayar; 59, 62: ID1974/Shutterstock.com, Everett Collection/Shutterstock. com; 60: Vladimirs Koskins/Shutterstock.com; 61: Kohls, Ulrich; 64: Aspen Photo/Shutterstock.com; 66: Laura Stone/ Shutterstock.com, rmnoa357/Shutterstock.com; 67: alexkatkov/Shutterstock.com; 68: Gerard McGovern, Peter23, Spyrosdrakopoulos, Adam.J.W.C., Nagyman, Los Angeles; 69: Samantha Bennett, Sergey Golotvin/Shutterstock.com;71: Michael C. Gray/Shutterstock.com; 73: Dmytro Vietrov/Shutterstock.com; 75: rmnoa357/Shutterstock.com; 76: Luigi Fardella/Shutterstock.com

Chapter number illustrations: zentilia/Shutterstock.com
White photo frame: hellena13/Shutterstock.com
Picture frames on the black bookshelf: S.V.Art/Shutterstock.com
Video player: Aleksandr Bryliaev/Shutterstock.com
Wood frames: Hilch/Shutterstock.com
Pennant: Nicholas 852/Shutterstock.com
Paper: RoyStudio.eu/Shutterstock.com, MaxyM/Shutterstock.com
Vintage paper: Theeradech Sanin/Shutterstock.com, LiliGraphie/Shutterstock.com, Picsfive/Shutterstock.com

INDEX

In this index, page numbers in ***bold italics*** font indicate photos or videos.

INDEX